SHELL-TURNING

MUNITION WORKER TURNING OUTSIDE OF A 4·5-IN. SHELL

SHELL-TURNING
for
Munition Workers

by

H. SCHOFIELD AND J. D. DRIVER

The Naval & Military Press Ltd

Published by

The Naval & Military Press Ltd
Unit 5 Riverside, Brambleside
Bellbrook Industrial Estate
Uckfield, East Sussex
TN22 1QQ England

Tel: +44 (0)1825 749494

www.naval-military-press.com
www.nmarchive.com

In reprinting in facsimile from the original, any imperfections are inevitably reproduced and the quality may fall short of modern type and cartographic standards.

PREFACE

An endeavour is here made to set forth, in plain language, and with simple diagrams, the work which faces the thousands of men and women who have volunteered for the business of munition-making.

The great majority of these volunteers have not even an elementary notion of engineering; probably do not distinguish a mil from a millimetre. The authors have therefore provided them with some preliminary instruction to assist them when they get to work in increasing the output of munitions.

When it is a case of "catching up", short cuts must be adopted. It is hoped that this handbook will save precious time, and give its readers some clear idea of what to do, and what a lathe can do.

The thanks of the authors are due to Messrs. Philip Harris & Co., and to Messrs. Alfred Herbert, Ltd., for kindly lending the blocks for several of the illustrations.

H. S.
J. F. D.

Contents

	Page
LATHES	9
SHELL-TURNING	17
GENERAL HINTS	27
CUTTING SPEEDS	29
CUTTING TOOLS	31
ENGINEERING MEASUREMENTS	37
MEASURING INSTRUMENTS	41

TABLES

	Page
DECIMAL EQUIVALENTS OF AN INCH	53
ENGLISH METRIC EQUIVALENTS	54
INDEX	55

SHELL-TURNING

LATHES

Lathes may be divided into three main classes:—

1. **Engine or general-purpose Lathes.**—These lathes are not designed for any special class of work, but are so made that they can deal with any ordinary castings or forgings of the type usually met with in an engineering works. For example, fly-wheels, pulleys, and shafting may be turned, as well as cylinders and similar engine parts bored out on such machines, which are generally also capable of being used for cutting internal and external threads. Such lathes require considerable skill for their operation, and for a machinist to be able to deal successfully with any class of work which comes along, means that he must have had a number of years of training in an engineering works. In no case should a man be

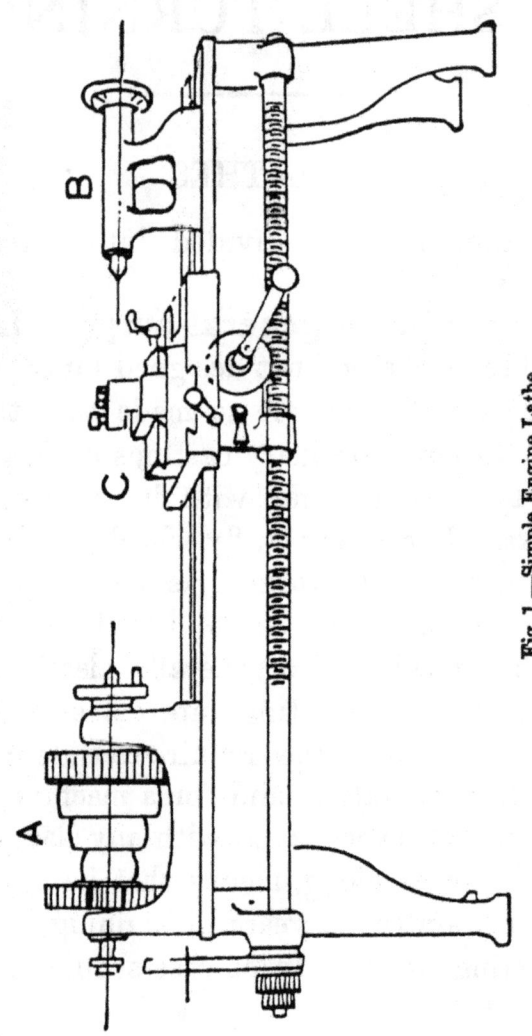

Fig. 1.—Simple Engine Lathe

Fig. 2.—MODERN ENGINE LATHE

LATHES

rated as a "turner" who has not had this experience.

Fig. 1 shows an engine lathe in its simplest possible form, and fig. 2 gives an illustration of a modern engine lathe.

A is the fast headstock.

B the loose headstock.

C is the saddle on which the cutting tools are mounted.

The driving belt comes from the overhead countershafting on to one or other of the pulleys on the fast headstock. The work to be turned is supported in various ways, depending upon its shape and size. The most common method is to support it between the centres of the fast and loose headstocks, as shown in fig. 3, which represents a piece of shafting held so that it may be turned on the outside; the carrier at the headstock end being necessary to rotate the shaft.

Before being placed in the lathes, countersunk centre holes are drilled into each end of the shaft. These are usually done by means of a special machine which ensures that the holes are *exactly* in the centre of the shaft.

When it is necessary to bore a piece of work, it is bolted to the face-plate of the lathe or

12   SHELL-TURNING

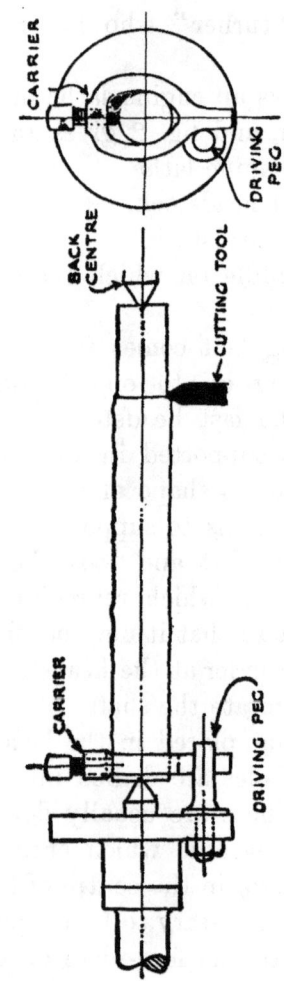

Fig. 3.—Turning Shaft supported between Centres

LATHES

held in the jaws of a chuck, as shown in fig. 4. A chuck suitable for this purpose is represented in fig. 5. (See plate p. 16.)

Very often it is necessary to bore, and after-

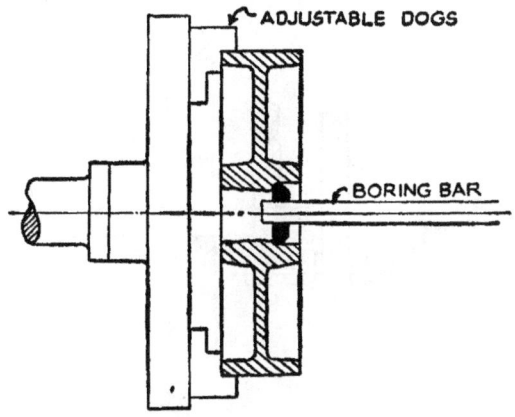

Fig. 4.—Boring Pulley held in Chuck

wards turn the same piece of work, in which case it is bored, and then removed from the face-plate and fitted on to a mandril of suitable size. A mandril consists of a turned steel bar having centre holes at each end, and of such a diameter that it will just fit the bored hole. They are generally turned very slightly tapered, so that they can be pushed into the bored hole until tight, thus ensuring a firm drive.

The mandril is then centered in the lathe in the ordinary way, and the outside of the work can be turned, as shown in fig. 6.

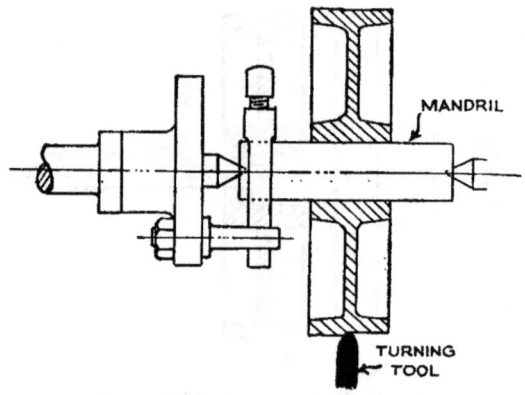

Fig. 6.—Turning Pulley supported on Mandril

There are, of course, other operations which are performed on lathes, but it is not necessary to describe them here.

2. An illustration of a **Semi-automatic Lathe** is given in fig. 7.

These differ from engine lathes in that they are more suitable for repetition work, such, for example, as the turning of bolts, &c. Gene-

Fig. 7.—SEMI-AUTOMATIC LATHE WITH SPECIALLY DESIGNED CUTTING TOOLS FOR GUN PARTS

rally the various cutters are arranged in a revolving "capstan" so that time may be saved in changing tools when performing various operations.

For some classes of work it is often convenient to make each piece out of a bar of metal. Therefore, the headstock is made hollow so that the metal may be fed through to the cutters as required.

For example, in making a simple bolt the process is somewhat as follows:—

First, a bar of steel, square or hexagonal in section (depending on whether square- or hexagon-headed bolts are required), is fed into the lathe; the length of the metal fed in will depend upon the length of bolt required to be made. One set of cutters then removes the metal from the body of the bolt, turning it at one setting to the correct diameter. Another set of cutters are then moved into position, and these turn the thread on the end of the bolt. The bolt is then finished by being parted off by means of another set of cutters. It will be seen by this brief description that once the various cutters are accurately set in position, little skill is required in the manipulation of such a lathe, the most important duties being confined to feeding the machine and changing the cutters between the operations.

3. **Automatic lathes** are similar in principle (see fig. 8), with the exception that, once adjusted and set in motion, they will continue to work until the supply of metal which they are "converting" is used up. Such lathes are very intricate in design, and the work of setting the cutters requires great skill; but once adjusted, a boy is able to look after several such machines, going from one to another to give it fresh supplies of metal and see that each machine is working satisfactorily.

Fig. 8.—AUTOMATIC LATHE

Fig. 5.—FOU

Fig. 9.—AUTOMATIC LATHE MACHINING BEVEL GEARS

AW CHUCK

SHELL-TURNING

At first sight it would appear that shell cases are very suitable for work in automatic or semi-automatic lathes. This is quite true; but the disadvantage of this procedure is the fact that considerable time and expense are needed to perfect a lathe for this rather exceptional engineering requirement. It is much better, therefore, to have the simplest possible kind of lathes and arrange so that each machine may easily perform one operation; the shell case being passed on from one machine to the other until the whole of the operations are performed.

It will be seen that by this arrangement the work is really of a semi-automatic character, each lathe being equivalent to one setting of the capstan lathe, the difference being that instead of the shell case being retained in the lathe and the cutters changed, it is transferred from one lathe to another, each lathe performing a different operation. In this manner a number of simple, and in many cases old-fashioned, "engine" lathes may be adapted to work very satisfactorily, and semi-skilled operators may be quickly trained to perform the various simple operations.

The various processes in the turning of shells depend somewhat on the size and type, but they are in general as follows:—

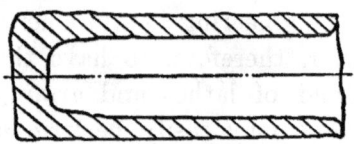

Fig. 10.—Section of Shell Case before Machining

The steel forging consists of a hollow cylindrical body stopped at one end, as shown in fig. 10.

This is required to be: (1) parted to length, (2) centered, (3) turned on the outside, (4) bored, (5) faced to the correct length, and (6) recessed.

Parting to Length.—The face at the open end is turned flat. This is performed by holding the shell case in some simple form of chuck, and traversing the cutter across the shell (fig. 11).

Centering.—The shell case is then trans-

SHELL-TURNING

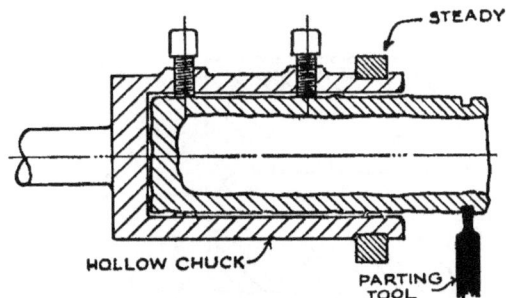

Fig. 11.—Parting to Length

ferred to a centering machine, in which it is held whilst a small hole is drilled in the centre of the blank end by means of a special cutter. The centre hole is intended to receive the pointed centre of the movable headstock, so that the shell case may be supported whilst the outside is turned down to size (fig. 12).

In this connection it should be

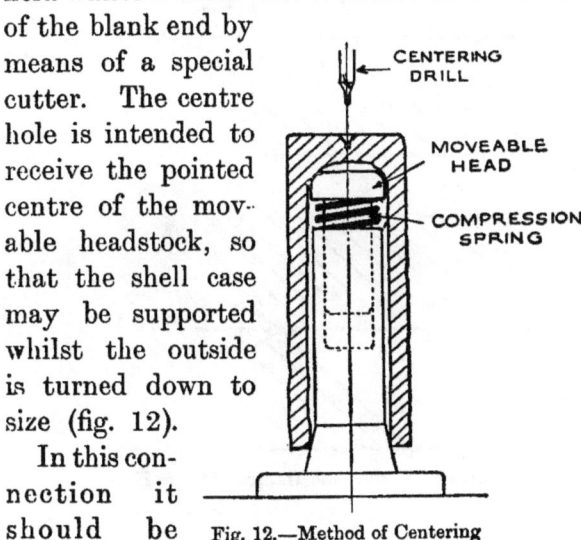

Fig. 12.—Method of Centering

20 SHELL-TURNING

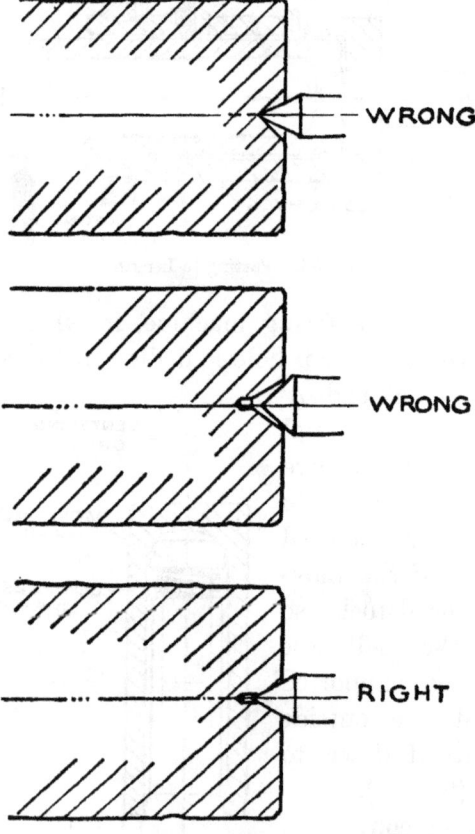

Fig. 13.—Correct and Incorrect Centre Holes

noticed that for smooth running the angle of taper of the centre hole should coincide with that of the pointed centres in the lathe headstocks (see fig. 13).

In no case should the point of the centre bear only on the bottom of the hole.

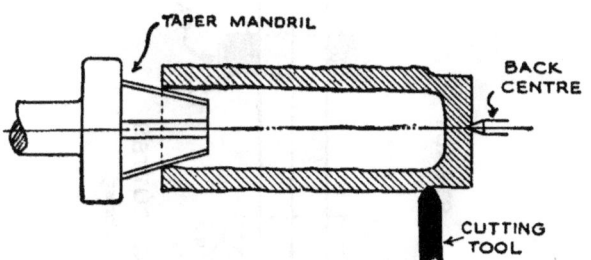

Fig. 14.—Turning Outer Surface

Turning.—After being centered the forging is turned on the outside. The method of supporting the work is by means of a tapered mandril, against which it is pressed by means of the centre of the loose headstock. The tapered mandril has three projecting steel keys which effectually serve to rotate the shell against the cutter. A common design for such a mandril is shown in fig. 14.

Boring.—When turned on the outside, the shell is held in an internal chuck, and bored out by means of a boring bar. The boring bar

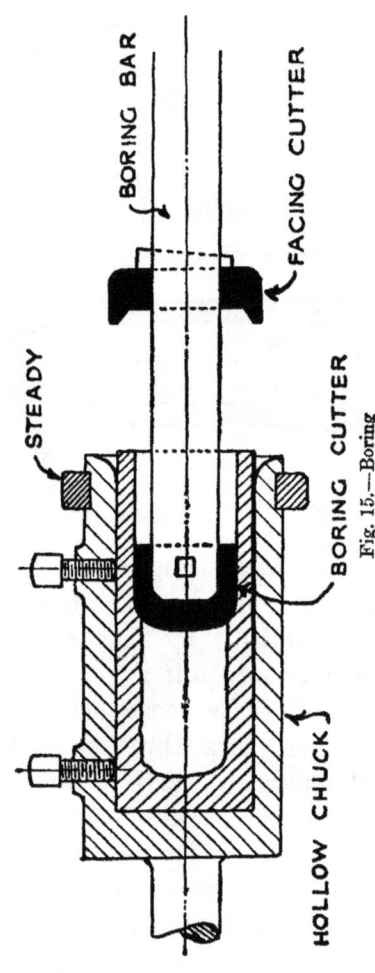

Fig. 15.—Boring

SHELL-TURNING

(fig. 15) has two cutters, one at the end, and the other at such a distance from the end that when the boring cutter is coming into operation the second cutter faces off the end of the shell.

Before the second cutter comes into opera-

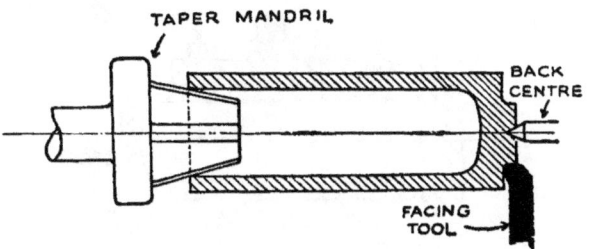

Fig. 16.—Facing

tion, the "feed" of the lathe should be disconnected and the boring bar traversed by hand. This is necessary because when boring against the solid end and also facing at the same time, the amount of cut would be excessive and probably break the cutters. In order to push the boring bar home it is best to bring the loose headstock against it from behind, and let the centre press the bar forward.

Facing.—The shell case is held between the loose headstock centre and a tapered mandril, as in operation 3, and the back end faced up so that the overall length is correct (fig. 16).

Recessing.—The shell case is held in a hollow chuck similar to the one used in operation 1, with the blank end facing outwards,

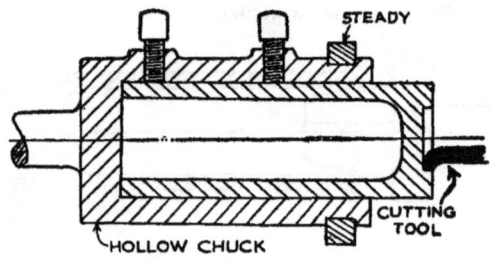

Fig. 17.—Recessing

and a cavity is then turned out of suitable size to receive a steel disc. Two cutting operations are necessary, the first to rough out the metal, and the second to finish to size with the base of the recess left perfectly flat and sharp at the corner.

It must be understood that there are many other processes, such as waving, profiling, &c., through which the shell must pass before completion; but as those previously mentioned are the important ones to which semi-skilled labour

SHELL-TURNING

is likely to be applied, it is unnecessary to proceed further.

In each operation the degree of accuracy must be within limits set by gauges. It must be borne in mind that skilled workmanship consists not only in performing the operation correctly to gauge, but also doing this rapidly; and the operator should always endeavour to work the machine to its utmost capacity, as then not only will more work be turned out in a given time, but also the work performed will be done with the greatest efficiency as regards the amount of power required to drive.

When working at high speeds and removing large quantities of metal, the cutters would, if allowed to work in a dry state, very soon get heated and dulled. It is necessary, therefore, to keep them flooded. A liquid poured on to the cut during the operation serves to cool the cutter and at the same time lubricate it, and when boring wash away the borings. This cutting compound consists usually of an emulsion of lard oil, soda, and water, and should be directed by means of a pipe right against the cutting edge of the tool; the larger the volume of liquid used the better.

GENERAL HINTS

The first care of the machinist should be to keep the lathe clean, well oiled, and properly adjusted. Never attempt to clean the machine when it is in motion.

Before commencing work on an unfamiliar machine, find out how the various motions are operated, and having mastered these details, discover how the machine is started and stopped.

It is exceedingly important that this latter detail should be carefully mastered, as sooner or later it will be necessary to stop the machine instantly if an accident or breakage is to be avoided.

When turning, with the work between the centres of the lathe, keep the centre in the loose headstock lubricated so as to avoid damaging the same by overheating.

Never wear clothing likely to get caught in the machinery or belting. Loose wristbands are a frequent cause of trouble or accident.

Avoid the habit of placing the hands on the

machine. Do not allow your attention to be diverted from your own machine when it is in motion.

If your clothing happens to get caught in the machinery do not attempt to pull or tear the material, but stop the lathe at once.

Do not work with blunt tools, but have them reground when necessary. There is one cutting angle suitable for the class of material being machined. This should be found and adhered to.

Always cut out feeding mechanism and withdraw cutter before stopping the lathe.

A well-arranged and sharp cutter pares the metal off, whereas a blunt one drags it off and leaves the surface of the work pitted.

If mysterious noises develop, stop the lathe and ascertain the cause.

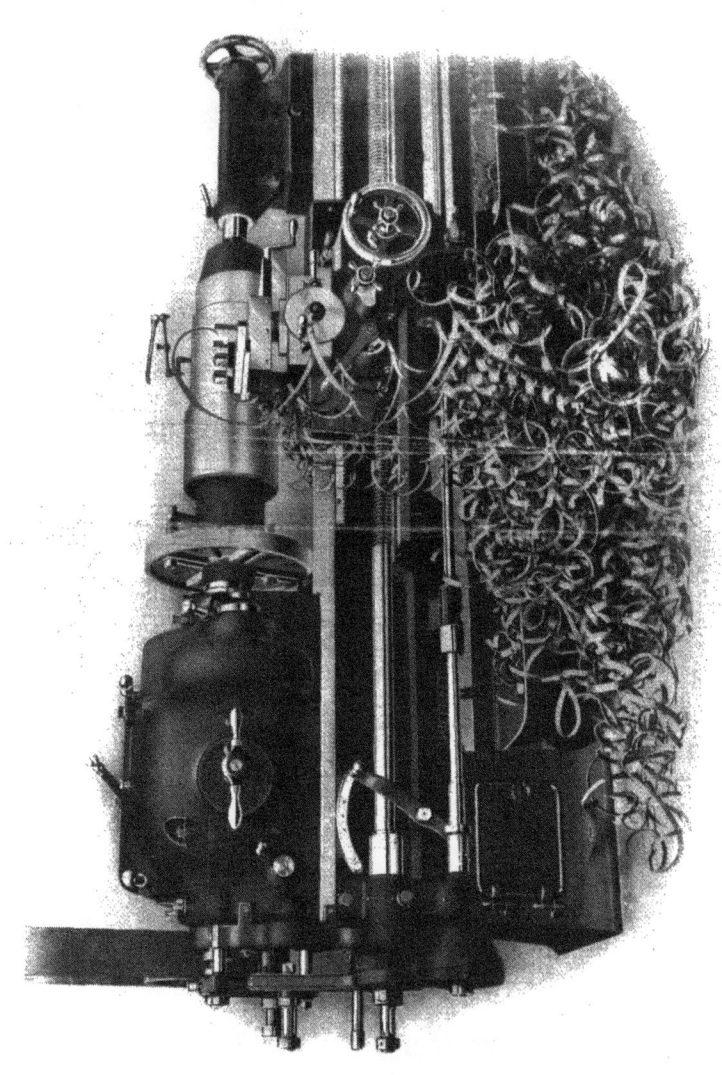

CUTTING SPEEDS

The average speed at which the metal being machined is passing the cutting tool is termed the "cutting speed". This varies with the metal, the depth and travel of the cut, and the quality of steel used for the cutter.

In practice the cutting speed varies from 25 to 100 feet per minute. It is economical to work at as high a speed as the cutting tool will stand without becoming blunted too rapidly.

To find the cutting speed, measure the diameter in inches before the cut and after; add these together and divide by 2 to find the mean diameter; multiply first by 3·14 or $3\frac{1}{7}$; then by the number of revolutions per minute made by the work. This result divided by 12 gives the cutting speed in feet per minute.

EXAMPLE.—

Diameter before cut = $4\frac{1}{4}$ inches.

Diameter after cut = 4 inches.

Mean diameter = $\dfrac{4\frac{1}{4} + 4}{2} = \dfrac{8\frac{1}{4}}{2} = 4\frac{1}{8}$ inches.

Speed of work, 50 revolutions per minute.

Then cutting speed = $\dfrac{4\frac{1}{8} \times 3\cdot14 \times 50}{12} =$ { 54 feet per minute.

The following table gives the approximate rate of revolution of different diameters of work to ensure a cutting speed of 40 feet per minute.

Mean Diameter.	Speed of Work per Minute.
3 inches.	50 revolutions.
4 ,,	39 ,,
5 ,,	31 ,,
6 ,,	26 ,,
8 ,,	19 ,,
10 ,,	15 ,,

To increase or decrease the cutting speed it is only necessary to alter the rate of revolution of the work in the same proportion.

CUTTING TOOLS

It is clear that the steel used for the turning tools must be harder than the material to be turned. Tool steels may be divided into

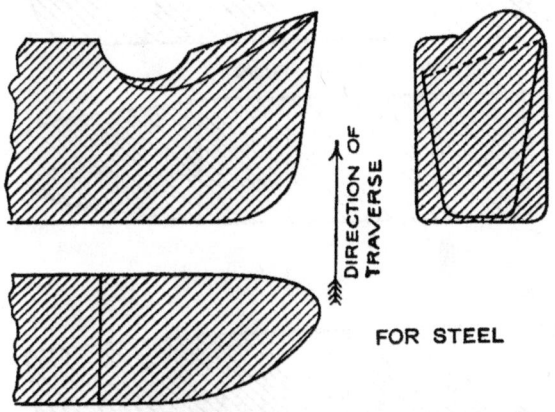

Fig. 19.—Shape of Cutting Tools (*see p. 32*)

(a) *High Carbon Steel*, which requires to be hardened and tempered, and (b) *Self-hardening Steel*.

This latter has recently been considerably improved, with the result that the permissible cutting speeds can be considerably increased,

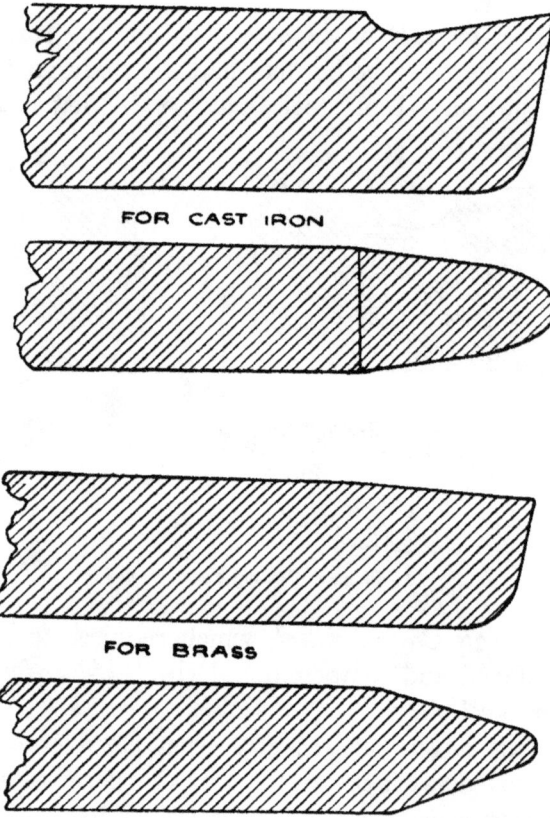

Fig. 19.—Shape of Cutting Tools (*see p 31*)

CUTTING TOOLS

and hence it has received the name "high-speed steel". Since shell forgings are generally of tough hard metal, high-speed steel is almost exclusively used for the roughing cuts.

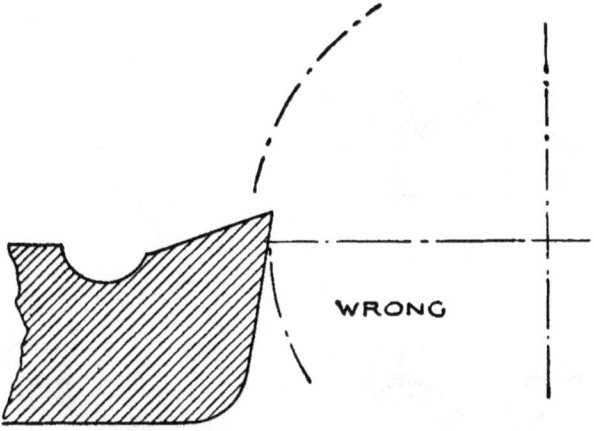

Fig. 20.—Setting the Cutting Tools (*see p. 34*)

Shape of Cutting Tools.—The shape of the tool depends upon the material which it is desired to work. Fig. 19 shows the best shapes of tool for working with brass, cast iron, and steel respectively.

Setting of Tools.—Fig. 20 shows the correct and incorrect positions for setting the tool relative to the work which it is to turn.

SHELL-TURNING

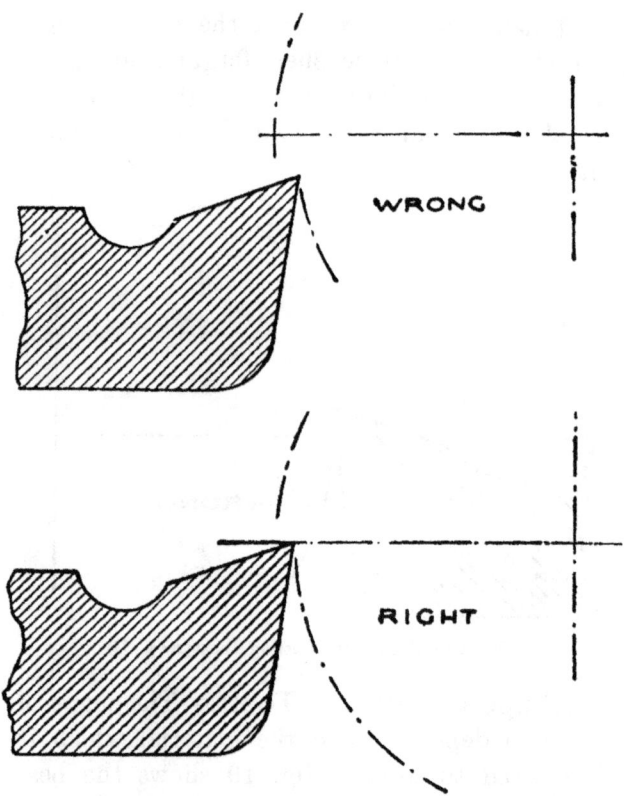

Fig. 20.—Setting the Cutting Tools (*see p. 33*)

It will be noticed that the cutting edge of the tool should coincide with level of the lathe centres.

CUTTING TOOLS

Regrinding Cutters.—When regrinding tools, it is important to retain as far as possible the original shape of the cutting edge.

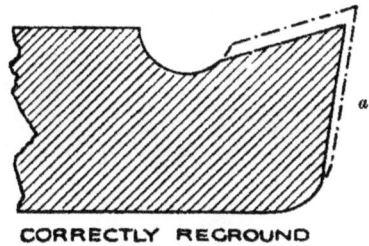

CORRECTLY REGROUND

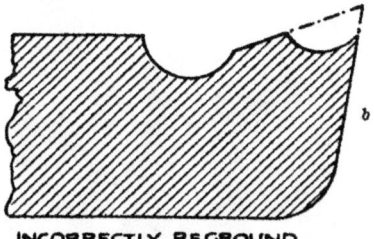

INCORRECTLY REGROUND

Fig. 21 (*a* and *b*).—Regrinding Cutters

Unless considerable care is exercised in this respect it is easy to adopt a careless method of grinding, shown in fig. 21 *b*. This saves some little time at the moment, but quickly renders the tool useless, and necessitates reforging.

ENGINEERING MEASUREMENTS

In many cases, portions of machinery have to be manufactured to a high degree of accuracy in order that the various parts may fit into one another when assembled together. As absolute accuracy is impossible, it is usual to state on the working drawings or instructions what are the limits of error which can be allowed. These limits are usually expressed in thousandths of an inch. Thus a shell may be required to be turned on the outside to a certain dimension within the limits of 10 one-thousandths of an inch; that is to say, the finished size must not be more than 5 thousandths of an inch above or below the dimension given.

In order to save time in measuring, limit gauges are often employed for this class of work.

Fig. 22 shows two types of limit gauge used in lathe work; one gauge being larger than the required dimensions, say by 5 one-thousandths, and the other gauge the same amount smaller.

It will be seen that if such a gauge is used, and the article turned down so that the larger size will go over it, but the smaller one will not, then the size of the article is within the limits of the gauge.

As the term "thousandth of an inch" is often

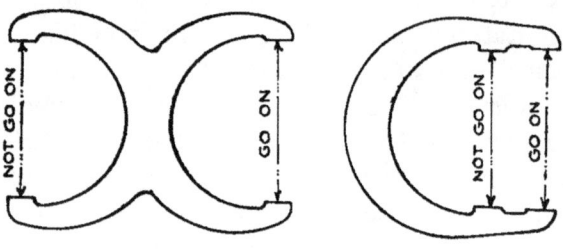

Fig. 22.—Limit Gauges

used, the name "mil" is given to it; thus if a piece of work is required by the drawing or instruction sheet to be turned to a diameter of 4 inches plus 5 mils, it means that the finished diameter must be 5 one-thousandths of an inch larger than 4 inches.

NOTE.—Care must be taken not to confuse the "mil" with the French dimension "millimetre".

At first sight it would appear that one thousandth of an inch is a very small figure; and though this is true, it is quite possible to machine up a piece of work to within this amount with ease.

In order to fix the dimension in one's mind, it may be noted that a cigarette paper is about one thousandth of an inch in thickness, whilst an ordinary sheet of note-paper is 5 one-thousandths of an inch. Therefore, if a sheet of note-paper is wrapped round a piece of shafting, the diameter over the shafting will be 10 mils larger than over the bare shaft.

It is very easy to set the cutter in a lathe to much less than the thickness of a sheet of note-paper!

MEASURING INSTRUMENTS

1. **Engineer's Callipers.**—An illustration of a pair of simple callipers is given in fig. 23. These are usually set to size by tapping the

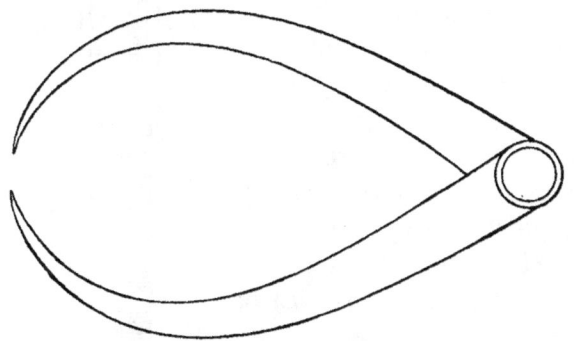

Fig. 23.—Simple Callipers

jaws against any part of the nearest machine frame.

They cannot be used for absolute measurement where accuracy is required, but they are very useful for comparing the size of any object with some standard similar object, or for transferring a measurement from one piece of work to another.

2. **Sliding Callipers.** — Sliding callipers are used to measure the thickness or diameter of any small object. They are graduated either according to the metric system or the English system.

If the metric system is used, the divisions will be in centimetres and millimetres; or if the English system is employed, they will be in inches and tenths of an inch. Greater accuracy is obtained by using the instrument in conjunction with a vernier.

The vernier consists of a second scale, placed alongside the fixed scale, and it

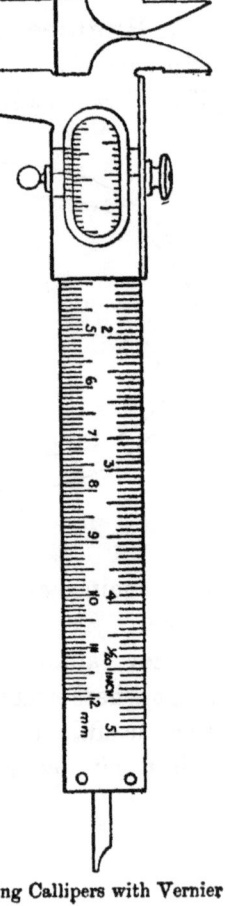

Fig. 24.—Sliding Callipers with Vernier

MEASURING INSTRUMENTS 43

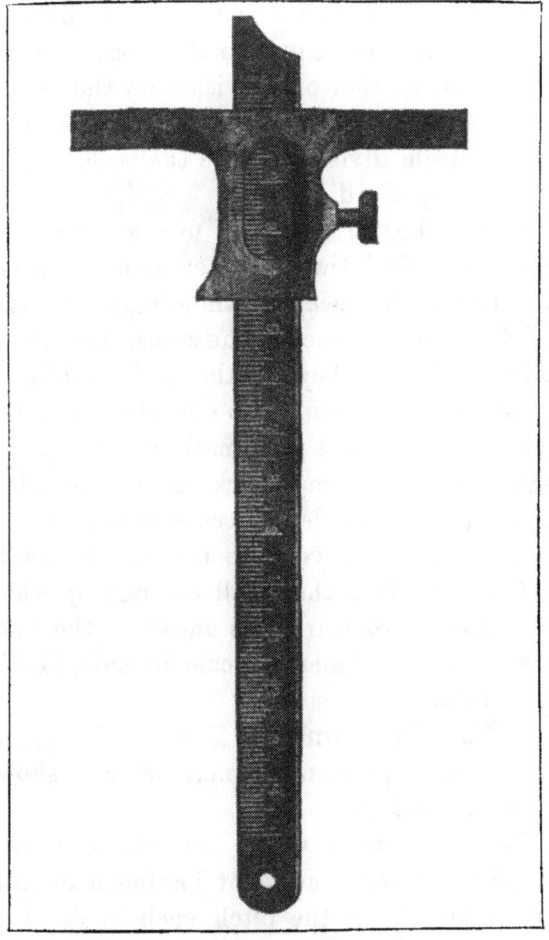

Fig. 25.—Sliding Callipers with Vernier

is graduated in such a way that 10 divisions on the vernier are equal to 9 divisions on the fixed scale, so that one division on the vernier is less than one division on the fixed scale by $\frac{1}{10}$ of a scale division, hence the scale may be read to $\frac{1}{100}$ of a division.

As an illustration of its use, suppose it is required to find the diameter of a rod which measures to the nearest whole mark 4 inches and 4 tenths of an inch. The zero of the vernier scale will be just beyond the 44th division in the scale. Now run your eye along the vernier until you find one mark which exactly corresponds with some mark on the fixed scale. Suppose this coincidence occurs at the mark 7, then the distance you are measuring will be 4·47 inches, since the small amount by which the vernier zero mark was ahead of the fixed zero mark is ·7 of a small-scale division, i.e. the next decimal place.

3. **The Micrometer Screw Gauge.**—The simplest pattern of micrometer is shown in figs. 26 and 27.

This instrument really consists of a very carefully cut screw and nut having a definite unit of length for the pitch, such as $\frac{1}{40}$ of an inch. The object to be measured is placed

MEASURING INSTRUMENTS 45

between the end of the screw and the projecting piece, and then the screw is adjusted by means of the milled head until the object is just lightly pressed between the two points.

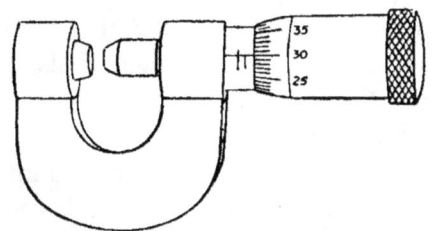

Fig. 26.—Micrometer Screw Gauge

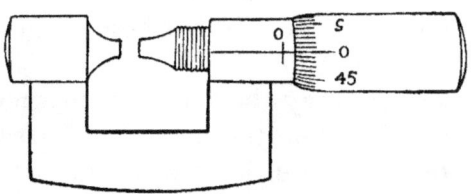

Fig. 27.—Micrometer Screw Gauge

Whole revolutions are read upon a flat scale engraved on the sleeve under the milled head, and fractions of a revolution are given by a scale placed round the edge of the milled head.

Suppose the pitch of the screw to be $\frac{1}{40}$ of an inch, then a scale of fortieths of inches is engraved on the spindle under the sleeve, and the milled head is circularly divided into 25 parts, each giving $\frac{1}{25}$ of $\frac{1}{40}$ of an inch, so that it would be possible to get a reading of the order $\frac{1}{1000}$ of an inch.

In using the screw gauge it is sometimes necessary to test the position of the zero, by screwing the two points into contact and noticing whether the circular scale is at 0. If this is not true, either (*a*) the amount of the zero error must be noted and allowed for in subsequent readings, or (*b*) the instrument must be set back to zero by means of a small screw provided in the head of the fixed jaw.

Care must always be taken not to screw the jaws together too tightly. This excess of pressure may injure the screw thread.

For measuring larger sizes of work a different pattern screw micrometer gauge of the form shown in fig. 28 is employed.

The movable pin A is attached to the thimble B at the milled end, and has a thread turned upon the portion which is concealed within the sleeve; if this is turned through 40 revolutions, the pin A will move one inch.

MEASURING INSTRUMENTS

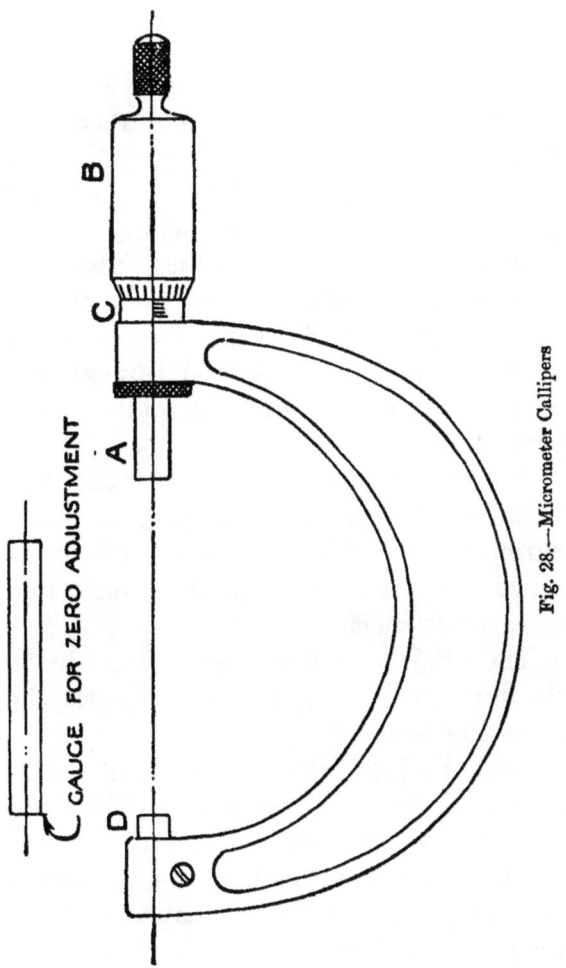

Fig. 28.—Micrometer Callipers

One turn of the thimble B therefore moves the pin A $\frac{1}{40}$ or $\frac{25}{1000}$ of an inch.

The graduations on the barrel C are forty to the inch, and therefore four turns of the thimble B moves the pin four of these divisions, that is to say, $\frac{4}{40}$ of an inch, which equals $\frac{1}{10}$ of an inch or 100 mils.

The bevelled edge of the thimble B is graduated into 25 divisions, and these are figured every fifth division: 0, 5, 10, 15, &c.

If the thimble B is turned through one of these divisions, it will have rotated $\frac{1}{25}$ of a revolution.

Now one complete revolution of the thimble B moves the pin A $\frac{1}{40}$ of an inch, therefore turning the thimble B through one division moves the pin A $\frac{1}{25}$ of $\frac{1}{40}$ of an inch, that is $\frac{1}{1000}$ of an inch.

The article to be measured is placed between the anvil D and the spindle A so that these just press on either side of it.

The opening between the anvil and the spindle is shown by the scale on the sleeve C and the bevelled portion of the thimble B.

To Read the Calliper. — Multiply the number of complete divisions visible on the scale of the barrel C by 25, and add the

MEASURING INSTRUMENTS

number of divisions on the bevelled edge of the thimble, from 0 to the line coincident with the base line of the graduation on the barrel C.

For example, suppose 6 complete divisions are shown on the scale of the barrel C and 4 on the bevelled edge of the thimble B. Multiply the 6 divisions on C by 25, which

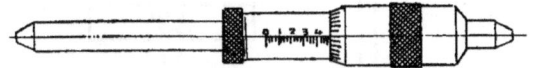

Fig. 29.—Internal Gauge with Micrometer

gives 150, and add the 4 divisions on B, giving a total of 154. That is to say, the jaws of the callipers are open $\frac{154}{1000}$ of an inch.

To reduce this result to a decimal, place the decimal point, counting from the right-hand side, after the third figure: thus, $\frac{154}{1000}$ = ·154.

If there had been 2 complete divisions shown on barrel C, and 16 on bevelled edge B, then the jaws would have been open, 2 × 25 = 50; together with the 16 divisions on bevelled edge of B making a total of 66 thousandths of an inch, that is, $\frac{66}{1000}$, which as a decimal is ·066, the 0 being added to make the third figure.

Gauges for measuring the diameter of holes

50 SHELL-TURNING

are also made on the same principle as shown in fig. 29.

The method of using them is just the same as in the previous case, with the exception

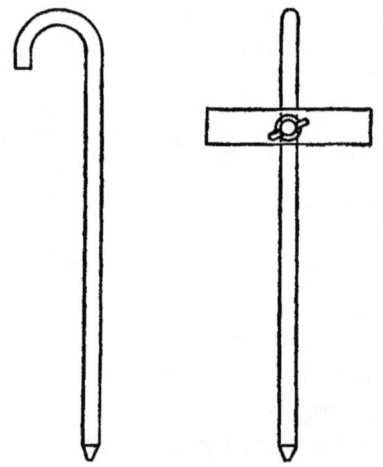

Figs. 30 and 31.—Depth Gauges

that when the scale is at 0, the gauge has a particular length (say 4 inches) between the points A and B, any alteration in the scale increasing this dimension accordingly.

4. **The Depth Gauge.** — Two common types of depth gauge are shown in figs. 30 and 31. The first is a fixed pattern, and this is

MEASURING INSTRUMENTS 51

the form generally used for testing the boring of shells. When the lip of the hooked end just rests on the machined edge of the shell, the lower pointer should be exactly in contact with the base of the hole.

Fig. 31 shows an adjustable type of gauge which can be set to mark any desired depth.

DECIMAL EQUIVALENTS OF AN INCH

To find the decimal equivalent of a fraction less than 1, divide the upper figure by the lower, placing the decimal point before the answer.

Thus: $\frac{1}{8}'' = 8\overline{)10}\ (\cdot 125 \quad = \cdot 125$ or 125 mils.
$$\begin{array}{r} 8 \\ \hline 20 \\ 16 \\ \hline 40 \\ 40 \\ \hline \end{array}$$

Fraction		Decimal equivalent
$\frac{1}{64}''$	=	·015625
$\frac{1}{32}''$	=	·03125
$\frac{3}{64}''$	=	·046875
$\frac{1}{16}''$	=	·0625
$\frac{1}{8}''$	=	·125
$\frac{3}{16}''$	=	·1875
$\frac{1}{4}''$	=	·250
$\frac{5}{16}''$	=	·3125
$\frac{3}{8}''$	=	·375
$\frac{7}{16}''$	=	·4375
$\frac{1}{2}''$	=	·50
$\frac{5}{8}''$	=	·625
$\frac{3}{4}''$	=	·75
$\frac{7}{8}''$	=	·875

ENGLISH METRIC EQUIVALENTS

The French unit of length is the centimetre. There are 2·54 centimetres in 1 inch; therefore, to convert centimetres to inches, divide by 2·54. To convert inches to centimetres, multiply by 2·54.

Inches.	Centimetres.	Centimetres.	Inches.
1	2·54	1	·394
2	5·08	2	·787
3	7·62	3	1·181
4	10·16	4	1·575
5	12·70	5	1·968
6	15·24	6	2·362
7	17·78	7	2·756
8	20·32	8	3·149
9	22·86	9	3·543
10	25·40	10	3·937

Index

Bolt-making, 15.
Boring, 21.

Callipers, engineer's, 41.
— how to read, 48.
— sliding, 42.
Carrier, 12.
Centering, 18.
Chuck, 13.
— hollow, 19.
Compression spring, 19.
Cutters, regrinding, 35.
Cutting compound, 25.
— speeds, 29.
— tools, 12, 31.
— — setting of, 33.
— — shape of, 33.

Dogs, adjustable, 13.
Driving peg, 12.

Face-plate, 11.
Facing, 23.

Gauge, micrometer screw, 44, 49.
Gauges, depth, 50.
— limit, 37.

Headstock, 11.
Hints, general, 27.

Instruments, 41.

Lathes, automatic, 16.
— engine, 9.
— semi-automatic, 14.

Mandril, 13.
— tapered, 21.
Measurements, 37.

Parting to length, 18.
— tool, 19.

Recessing, 24.
Revolution, rate of, 30.

Saddle, 11.
Shell case, 18.
— -turning, 17.

Turning, 21.
— tool, 14.

Vernier, 42.

www.ingramcontent.com/pod-product-compliance
Lightning Source LLC
Chambersburg PA
CBHW061343040426
42444CB00011B/3054